BRANCH LINES AROUND CROMER

Richard Adderson
and Graham Kenworthy

Series editor Vic Mitchell

MP Middleton Press

Cover picture: This is described in caption 50.

First Published November 1998
Reprinted July 1999
Second Reprint February 2001
Third Reprint October 2004

ISBN 1 901706 26 5

Design   Deborah Esher
Typesetting   Barbara Mitchell

Published by
        Middleton Press
        Easebourne Lane
        Midhurst, West Sussex
        GU29 9AZ
Tel: 01730 813169
Fax: 01730 812601
Email: info@middletonpress.co.uk
www..middletonpress.co.uk

Printed & bound by Biddles Ltd, Kings Lynn

CONTENTS

INDEX

Routes around Cromer in 1922. Although Cromer Beach was so named from its opening, Cromer High, North Walsham Main and North Walsham Town did not receive their identifying suffixes until after Nationalisation in 1948. To avoid confusion, these later names have been used throughout. (Dr. R.Joby)

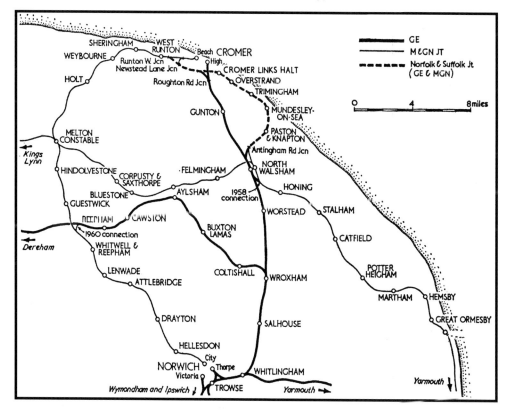

ACKNOWLEDGEMENTS

In addition to the photographers acknowledged in the photographic credits, we are most grateful to the following people for their assistance in the compilation of this book: L.Brooks, N.Digby, A.G.W.Garraway, B.Hunt, M.Howard, R.Meek, M.Rayner, R.Rivett, F.Shuttleworth, M.Storey-Smith, G.Thirst, R.Thorne, J.Watling and Mrs P.Youngman.

Readers of this book may be interested to know of the following societies: Great Eastern Railway Society (Membership Secretary J.R.Tant, 9 Clare Road, Leytonstone, London E11 1JU) and the Midland & Great Northern Circle (Membership Secretary G.L.Kenworthy, 16 Beverley Road, Brundall, Norwich NR13 5QS)

GEOGRAPHICAL SETTING

Everyone who has never been to Norfolk will tell you that it is flat. This is true in the extreme west of the county where it extends into the fens, but the statement is certainly not true of the area around Cromer and Sheringham. In fact, the highest point in the entire county is to be found just south of West Runton, barely one mile from the sea. The high ground on which this point is located is referred to as the Holt-Cromer Ridge, which, as the name suggests, is at its most prominent between those two towns.

This physical barrier, lying east-west, presented a problem to the promoters and builders of the East Norfolk Railway, which approached Cromer from the south. From the North Walsham direction the line started climbing the southern slope of the Ridge just south of Gunton. In the event, a combination of local opposition, which did not want the railway too close to the town, and a lack of financial resources, which meant that expensive earthworks were out of the question, dictated that the first terminus would sit on top of the Ridge. From here there was a superb, but rather distant, view of the town that

it claimed to serve.

By contrast, the Midland & Great Northern Joint route from the west reach-ed Cromer via the strip of land between the Ridge and the coast, albeit on top of the sea cliffs. However, as the gradient diagram shows, even this route required three steep gradients between Melton Constable and Sheringham. These were necessary in order, first of all, to descend from the high ground at Melton into the Glaven Valley, and then to cross the western shoulder of the Ridge, before the relatively level run along the cliff-top to Cromer.

The final approach to Cromer, the Norfolk & Suffolk Joint via Mundesley, dropped quickly from North Walsham into the valley of the River Ant. It then climbed by an undulating route up the eastern shoulder of the Ridge; this required some fairly heavy earthworks and substantial bridges. The summit of the branch was reached close to the point where it tunnelled under the East Norfolk route before taking an oblique, but steep, course down the north face of the Ridge in order to meet up with the M&GN line at the Runton Junctions.

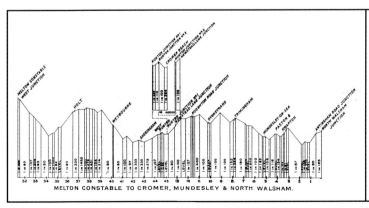

MELTON CONSTABLE TO CROMER, MUNDESLEY & NORTH WALSHAM.

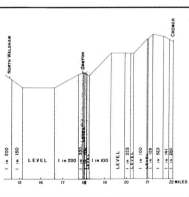

HISTORICAL BACKGROUND

Railways came relatively late to the North-east "quadrant" of Norfolk. The first railway in the county was opened in 1844 and ran virtually due east from Norwich via Reedham to Yarmouth. The north coast was reached by a line which ran almost due north from Wymondham (nine miles west of Norwich) to Wells in 1857. Cromer, however, had to wait another twenty years before the first railway contact was made with the outside world, despite the fact that the first East Norfolk Railway Act, for the line from Whitlingham Junction, on the eastern outskirts of Norwich, to North Walsham, had been passed in 1864, two years after the formation of the Great Eastern Railway. The delay was due to a major crisis in the financial world in 1866, and the line eventually opened in sections, as far as North Walsham on 20th October 1874, to Gunton on 29th July 1876 and to Cromer on 26th March 1877.

Meanwhile, other influences had been at work, approaching the Sheringham and Cromer area from the west of the county. Between 1879 and 1882, Melton Constable (only 11 miles from Sheringham and 15 from Cromer) was reached from King's Lynn by the Lynn and Fakenham Railway. The ultimate objective of this route was Norwich and so, having reached Melton Constable from Fakenham, the main route veered south-east, away from the coast; however, the same authorising Act also made provision for a branch from Melton Constable towards Sheringham. But the Company's immediate priority was to complete the link with the Yarmouth & North Norfolk Railway, which had reached North Walsham from Great Yarmouth in June 1881. This connection opened on 5th April 1883, some three months after the Lynn & Fakenham, the Yarmouth & North Norfolk and other smaller companies had amalgamated to form the Eastern & Midland Railway.

These events delayed construction of the route to Holt somewhat, and the line was eventually opened to a temporary terminus in the town on 1st October 1884. The Directors of the new company decided that they could not afford to use external contractors for new construction, and that any further work would have to be carried out using their own labour force and equipment. Following this decision, progress towards Cromer was halted early in 1885 due to the deployment of these resources to other, more strategically important, work elsewhere on the system. Once this other work was complete, the labour force returned and work restarted on the Cromer extension, which opened to passengers on 16th June 1887; the station name Cromer Beach was used from the beginning. The substantial intermediate station at Sheringham (spelt "Sherringham" until the mid-1890s) was opened at the same time but, following comments from the Board of Trade's Inspector, the opening of the rather rudimentary station at West Runton was delayed until September. Weybourne was not opened until 1st July 1901.

The third and final part of the north-east Norfolk jig-saw was also a disproportionate time in its development. An E&M Act of 1888 authorised the construction of a line from that company's North Walsham station to Mundesley, together with a connection and GER running powers from the East Norfolk line, but financial difficulties prevented its being started. Extra time for completion of the line was granted by the Act of 1893 which vested the E&M in both the Midland and the Great Northern Railway Companies. This action brought about the formation of the Midland & Great Northern Joint Committee, which was to remain independent until 1936.

The GER co-operated with both parent companies and the two organisations soon went into partnership to build and open the branch to Mundesley, a task which was completed when the line, with its one intermediate station at Paston and Knapton, opened on 1st July 1898. In the same year the Norfolk & Suffolk Joint Committee (half GER and half M&GN) was formed to administer the line, together with the extension along the coast to Cromer. This line, from Mundesley to Roughton Road Junction, with stations at Trimingham and Overstrand, was opened on 3rd August 1906. A few days earlier, on 23rd July, the connection from Cromer Junction (GER) to Runton East Junction and the avoiding curve between Newstead Lane Junction and Runton West Junction had been opened.

As already mentioned, the Grouping of 1923 left the M&GN and, therefore, the N&S

Joint Committees independent, but the GER was absorbed into the London & North Eastern Railway. The LNER finally took over administration of the M&GN and the N&S on 1st October 1936. All the routes became part of the Eastern Region of British Railways in 1948.

At this time all the lines and stations were still open, but this happy situation began to change in 1953, with the complete closure, on 6th April, of the line from Mundesley to Roughton Road Junction. Rationalisation of passenger facilities at Cromer took place in 1954 when Cromer High closed to passengers on 20th September, following improvements to the more conveniently sited Beach station. It did, however, remain open for freight until 7th March 1960.

North Walsham Town succumbed, together with most of the M&GN Section on 28th February 1959, and the Newstead Lane to Runton West Junction spur closed completely in April 1963.

1964 brought the loss of passenger services between Sheringham and Melton Constable on 6th April and from North Walsham to Mundesley on 5th October. Both sections, along with that from Cromer to Sheringham, saw continued use for freight until 28th December of that year; freight facilities were further reduced when the service beyond North Walsham ceased on 31st January 1969. All remaining stations became unstaffed halts from 2nd January 1967, with tickets being issued by conductor-guards on the trains.

Soon after the BR closure west of Sheringham, the M&GN Preservation Society started negotiations to preserve the route as far as Holt. However, for some years the line was in limbo, and, during this time, trains were only allowed to carry members of the Society. The North Norfolk Railway's preserved line from Sheringham to Weybourne was finally opened to members of the public on 13th July 1975, following a public enquiry, the granting of a Light Railway Order (to BR in the first instance) and detailed inspections. The Light Railway Transfer Order was made by the Department of the Environment in 1976, since when the NNR has been wholly responsible for the operation of the railway. The preserved line was extended to a temporary terminus at Kelling Camp in late August 1983 and the extension to Holt followed in 1988, the new terminus being about one mile short of the original station due to the construction of the Holt bypass.

PASSENGER SERVICES

As the area around Cromer is a holiday area, summer timetables have been quoted, where available, to illustrate the level of services provided. However, to avoid unnecessarily complicated details, weekday trains running on less than five of those days have been excluded. Also excluded are short workings (i.e. those not covering the full length of a particular line) unless they are relevant to the overall picture.

1877 to 1906

Prior to 1906 the situation was quite simple as the only services in existence were unconnected and, therefore, self-contained; the only complication arose in 1898, from which date Mundesley was served by trains from both stations at North Walsham.

NORTH WALSHAM TO CROMER

The November 1884 timetable showed a weekday service of seven passenger trains between North Walsham and Cromer; there were only two trains on a Sunday. All originated at Norwich. Few of these trains were regarded as providing any more than a local service, connections from London providing an overall journey time of around five hours.

The summer service, as might be expected, was more generous, the August 1887 Bradshaw indicating ten weekday trains, with four on Sundays.

There was little, if any, change following the arrival of the Eastern & Midland Railway at Cromer Beach Station in 1887. However, the last ten years of the century saw a dramatic increase in competition, particularly where longer distance traffic was concerned. Cromer was developing as a fashionable seaside resort and the Great Northern Railway arm of the M&GN Committee had identified the potential for through traffic to Cromer from London via Peterborough. The GER had to compete and, following an 1895 trial run, non-stop from Liverpool Street to North Walsham, the "Cromer Express" was introduced on 1st July 1897, running to Cromer in under three hours from the capital.

MELTON CONSTABLE TO CROMER BEACH

In September 1885, Holt had six trains on weekdays reversing there, while it was a terminus. In August 1887 there were seven weekday trains and three on Sundays to Cromer Beach; the weekday trains called at both Holt and Sheringham (the only intermediate stations at this date), but only the first Sunday train did so; the second ran non-stop, while the third called intermediately by request only.

By July, 1892 the service was much the same, but two of the weekday services carried through coaches from Kings Cross. The 2.30 p.m. service took just over four hours from London and was described in the timetable as "Special Cromer Express", indicating the importance attached to the Cromer traffic by the GNR.

However by 1903, weekday services had increased to fourteen, further supporting the rapidly increasing popularity of the seaside's attractions. Four Sunday trains to Cromer, three of them in the early afternoon, with one from Norwich passing through Melton Constable non-stop, were provided.

NORTH WALSHAM TO MUNDESLEY

From its opening in 1898 the branch was provided with an initial summer service of sixteen weekday trains, nine GE and seven M&GN, with six (three each) on Sundays.

1906 to 1953

With such a complexity of lines, junctions and owning companies, the train services on the individual branches between the completion of the local network in 1906 and the first closure in 1953 were very closely linked and, in a number of cases, overlapped. Although not easily segregated, the following is a summary.

NORTH WALSHAM TO CROMER HIGH

The "Cromer Express" was renamed the "Norfolk Coast Express" from 1907 in recognition of the fact that it now carried three portions and divided at North Walsham. The first portion ran to the GER's Cromer station, the second following a few minutes later as far as Cromer Junction where it took the newly opened link via Roughton Road Junction, Newstead Lane Junction and Runton West Junction to West Runton and Sheringham. The third portion made its way via the Norfolk & Suffolk Joint Line through Mundesley, Trimingham and Overstrand.

By September 1913, the number of weekday trains between North Walsham and Cromer by the GER route had been increased to sixteen, five of which were designated "express passenger". Five stopped at Cromer Junction to detach portions for West Runton and Sheringham. The "Norfolk Coast Express" continued to run in three portions from North Walsham as detailed above.

There was a slight reduction in the number of services following World War I but there was a gradual recovery through the 1920s and 1930s so that by the Summer of 1938 there were fifteen weekday trains between North Walsham and Cromer, eleven of them detaching a West Runton/Sheringham portion (avoiding Cromer Beach) at Cromer Junction. The corresponding figures for Sundays were eight and two. Four of the weekday trains and two of those on Sunday were through workings from Liverpool Street, each of which included a restaurant car.

There was a similar pattern of reduction and recovery during and following World War II. In the Summer of 1950 there were fourteen weekday and four Sunday services; half of the weekday services were through workings from Liverpool Street, five of them including restaurant cars. This total included the "Norfolkman", a name introduced in 1948, and the "Broadsman", first seen in 1950.

NORTH WALSHAM TO CROMER BEACH VIA MUNDESLEY

In the Summer of 1913 there were fourteen trains between North Walsham and Mundesley, five M&GN and nine GE. All of the M&GN

trains ran through to Cromer Beach. Two of the GE trains ran through to Sheringham via the Runton Curve, while six terminated at Overstrand and one at Mundesley. There were a number of other M&GN trains working into Cromer Beach originating at both Mundesley and Overstrand. There were no through trains between North Walsham and Cromer Beach or Sheringham by this route on Sundays. Indeed Cromer Beach saw only an early afternoon train to Overstrand and the return working in time for tea.

By the Summer of 1938 the pattern of services had changed somewhat. Of eleven weekday trains originating at North Walsham, eight worked through to Cromer Beach (two of these started from North Walsham Town), one terminated at Overstrand and two at Mundesley. One other train to Cromer Beach started from Mundesley. Cromer Beach was closed on Sundays.

The 1950 timetable showed four through weekday trains from North Walsham to Cromer Beach plus three others (two to Sheringham and one to Holt) using the Runton Curve, while a further four terminated at Mundesley. All of these started from North Walsham Main. Cromer Beach was still a no-go area on Sundays.

MELTON CONSTABLE TO CROMER BEACH

In the Summer of 1911 there were twelve weekday trains, (half of which originated from west of Melton) with three on Sundays. In addition, two GER trains ran on weekdays from Sheringham to Cromer High via the Runton Curve and Cromer Junction.

By 1938 there were ten weekday through trains from Melton to Cromer Beach; there was also one through working to Cromer High using the propelling movement from Cromer Junction mentioned elsewhere. This operation was also carried out on seven daily through workings from Sheringham to Cromer High. There were still no Sunday trains at Cromer Beach, although it was possible to travel to Cromer High by one train from Sheringham and West Runton

The level of weekday service over the full branch in 1950 remained at the pre-war figure of ten, but by then there were also four workings through from Melton Constable to Cromer High *en route* to Norwich. The only Sunday service

from this direction serving Cromer continued to be the one train from Sheringham and West Runton to Cromer High.

1954 to 1998

After the Mundesley to Roughton Road Junction closure in 1953, followed swiftly by that of Cromer High in 1954, a relatively straightforward pattern resumed. The closure of virtually the whole of the M&GN system in 1959 and the truncations of 1964 simplified matters further and have meant that services have seen few dramatic changes since then.

NORTH WALSHAM AND MELTON CONSTABLE TO CROMER BEACH (1954-1964)

The Summer 1957 timetable showed a total of fifteen weekday services from North Walsham to Cromer Beach, five of which originated at Liverpool Street. Sunday saw four trains, all of a local nature. During the same period there were eleven weekday trains to Cromer from Melton Constable, plus another six from Sheringham. On Sundays, Melton Constable had no trains, but there were two from Holt to Cromer (both working through to London), with a third starting at Sheringham. However, pre-war independence continued to have its influence in that two separate tables had to be consulted to make sure of full details of the service between Sheringham and Cromer.

By the Summer of 1962, the closure of the M&GN lines meant that the timetable anomaly had been sorted out, with Melton Constable now being the terminus of the passenger service from North Walsham. Fourteen trains ran between North Walsham Main and Cromer before continuing to Sheringham and, in the majority of cases, to Melton Constable. By this time all weekday through services from London had ceased. There were four Sunday trains from North Walsham to Cromer Beach, three of which continued to and returned from Sheringham; there were no Sunday services beyond Sheringham.

NORTH WALSHAM TO MUNDESLEY (1954-1964)

Although by this time the route onward to Cromer had been severed, the residual service prior to closure is worth recording. By 1962 there were twelve weekday and four Sunday return services.

NORTH WALSHAM TO CROMER AND SHERINGHAM (1964-1998)

Ever since the closure of the Sheringham to Melton Constable section in 1964, the figure of around fourteen weekday and three or four Sunday services has remained fairly consistent over the years, apart from relatively slight variations in stopping patterns. The revival of a weekday through service from London to Cromer and Sheringham in 1997, albeit as a very early morning departure from the capital at 06.20, was, hopefully, a sign of improvements to come.

EAST NORFOLK.—Great Eastern.

MELTON CONSTABLE, SHERINGHAM, and CROMER (M. & G. N.)

July 1878

January 1943

NORWICH (Thorpe), WROXHAM, NORTH WALSHAM, MUNDESLEY-ON-SEA, CROMER, and SHERINGHAM

NORTH WALSHAM, OVERSTRAND, and CROMER (Beach)

1. Melton Constable to Cromer Beach

MELTON CONSTABLE

This 1906 plan shows the west end of the station with its single island platform. The M&GN "main line" from the west appears at the left and the "branch" to Cromer veers away at the top, demonstrating how through trains had to reverse direction

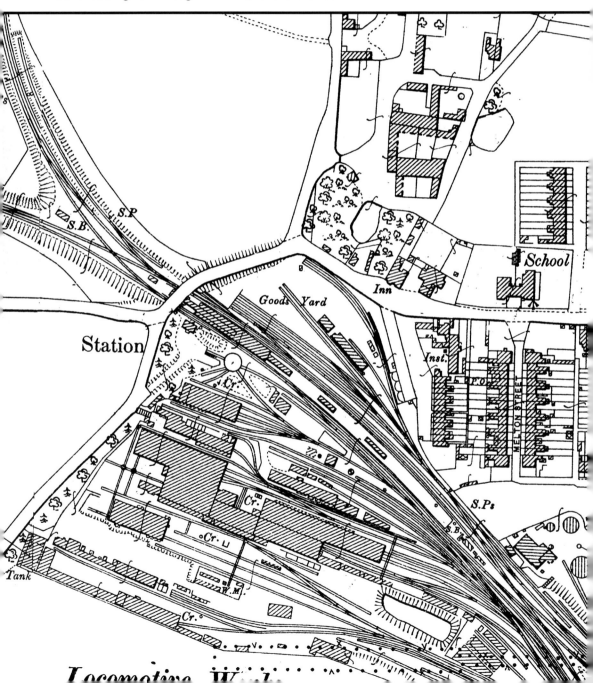

1.   Work was well advanced on the construction of the railway in 1881. In this view looking eastward the island platform and the goods shed are taking shape, while the trees in the middle distance will soon be swept away to make way for rows of terraced housing. An old cross-roads sign is still standing amidst the building materials, a reminder that the road layout had to be realigned to make way for the railway. (Marriott Coll./M&GN Circle)

(A 159.)

E. & M. R.

WEST RUNTON.

2.   Class F6 2-4-2T no. 67225 drifts round the sharp curve from the Cromer line into the station on 25th July 1953 with a typical local train of the period. In the foreground are the lines to South Lynn, which the milepost tells us is 31 miles away. (B.Harrison)

(A 159.)

E. & M. R.

—

Cromer Beach.

(18—V19)

MIDLAND & GREAT NORTHERN RAILWAYS JOINT COMMITTEE.

TO

Sheringham

3.   Following the main M&GN closure, Melton Constable lingered on for some five years as the terminus of a branch line from Sheringham before becoming a victim of the Beeching report. With the abandoned turntable pit to the left, the 2.56 p.m. to Norwich awaits departure time on the last day, 4th April 1964. Under the canopy the original spandrels with the initials CNR cast into them contrast with the modern electric lighting which was not installed until after the main line had been closed, and which was condemned locally as a sad waste of money. The spandrels reflect greater thrift, as they were utilised by the E&M after being cast for the projected Central Norfolk Railway, which never came into being. (R.J.Adderson)

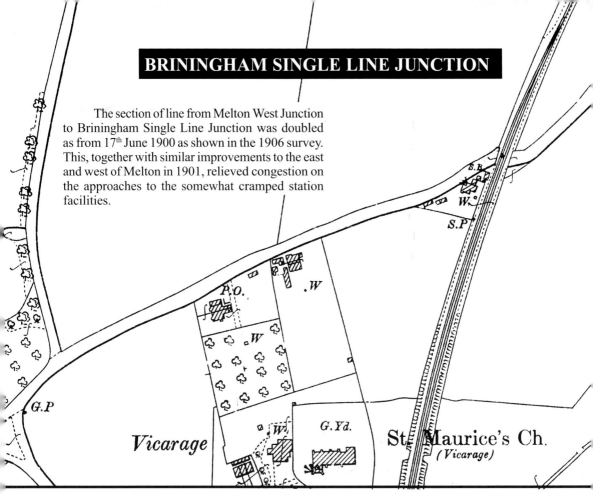

BRININGHAM SINGLE LINE JUNCTION

The section of line from Melton West Junction to Briningham Single Line Junction was doubled as from 17th June 1900 as shown in the 1906 survey. This, together with similar improvements to the east and west of Melton in 1901, relieved congestion on the approaches to the somewhat cramped station facilities.

S.B.

W.

S.P.

P.O.

.W

.W

G.P

Vicarage

G.Yd.

W

St. Maurice's Ch.
(Vicarage)

4. The photographer has scaled the signal post to record the rural scene here, looking northwards across the countryside towards Holt in 1959. With no houses in sight, the fields and single-track railway provide a contrast with nearby Melton Constable, whose industrial atmosphere earned it the description of "The Crewe of North Norfolk". (Ted Tuddenham/Peter J Bower and M&GN Circle).

5.   An M&GN Class C 4-4-0 approaches the signal box with a northbound train during the 1930s, passing the vantage point for the previous picture. The Whittaker tablet exchange apparatus is extended from the tender, ready to collect the tablet for the single line to Holt. Introduced in 1906, this equipment was invaluable on the M&GN, obviating the need to slow down for tablet exchange purposes on the many single track sections. (J.E.Levick)

6.   Half way between Briningham and Holt the line entered the hilly countryside of the Cromer ridge. This can clearly be seen as class B1 4-6-0 no. 61317 heads north with a local train from Melton Constable on 18th July 1958. (Ted Tuddenham/Peter J Bower and M&GN Circle).

HOLT

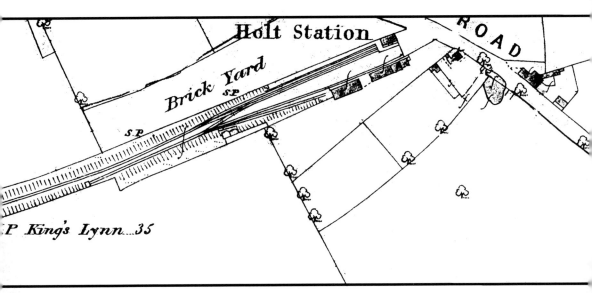

This 1886 plan indicates the existence of the terminus as opened in October 1884, although it appears to lack run-round facilities.

The 1906 survey shows the completed station together with the adjacent ballast pit from which stone was being extracted by 1899. The pit sidings continued to be operational until at least February 1959. The connection was controlled from Holt signal box.

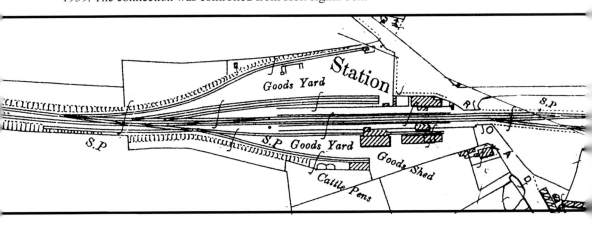

7.   A fire in March 1926 destroyed much of the original station building. It was rebuilt using concrete materials produced by the M&GN at Melton Constable and this view looking south clearly shows the concrete bricks and window frames used in the reconstruction. (R.F.Bonny)

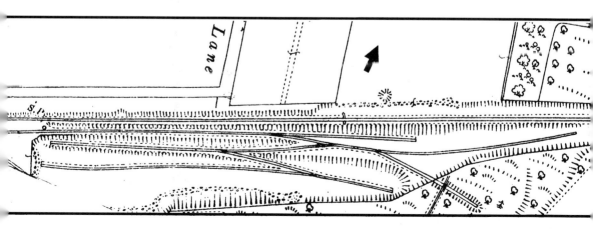

8.   The M&GN encouraged its staff to undertake first aid training, albeit on a largely voluntary basis, and the annual competitions for the Ambulance Cup and Shield were keenly contested by teams representing individual stations. This team from the Holt traffic department, if not illustrating the seven ages of man, certainly covered a wide range of age groups. Although extended to cover a wider area, the competition was perpetuated well into BR days, with some of the original M&GN trophies as the prizes. (Percy A Youngman Coll./M&GN Circle)

9.   Class A 4-4-0 no. 31 stands in the up platform with a short passenger train. Judging from the bogie coaches the train is probably the Cromer portion of an express to the Midlands, which will combine with the main section from Yarmouth at Melton Constable. The loco was nearly fifty years old when this picture was taken in the early 1930s. (J.E.Levick)

10.   During the early 1930s, the Holt pick up goods was often worked by a locomotive running-in after attention at Melton Works. This accounts for the use of a gleaming class C 4-4-0 passenger locomotive, no. 50, on this humble duty. Two private owner coal wagons can be seen in the sidings. (J.E.Levick)

11.   Two railwaymen loading a barrow provide the only signs of life as a diesel unit waits to continue its journey to Melton Constable and ultimately Norwich (City) on 28th February 1959. As in the previous picture, the distinctive M&GN criss-cross fencing casts its shadow across the platform. (A.E.Bennett)

HOLT BALLAST PIT

12.   Pits at Holt and neighbouring Kelling provided ballast for the line. The extent of the excavations at Holt in the 1930s is evident in this picture, as a passenger train heads south, behind an unrebuilt Class C 4-4-0. (J.E.Levick)

1937 Appendix

KELLING HEATH SIDINGS.

The points are controlled by Train Tablet and can be operated by either Up or Down trains.

Guards of trains requiring to use the Siding must, before entering the section, obtain the keys of the Cabin and Ground frame from the Signalman at Holt or Weybourne as the case may be.

The special attention of Guards and others is called to the necessity of using all due care whilst shunting wagons into and out of the above Siding, on account of the gradients, and wagon brakes must, when necessary, be pinned down.

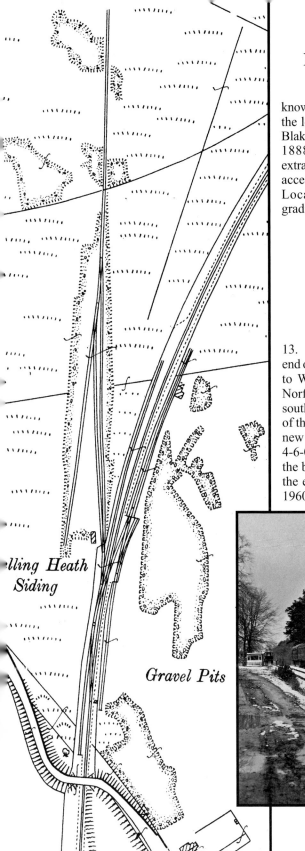

NORTH EAST OF HOLT

The site shown on the 1906 survey was known as Kelling Ballast Pit and was to have been the location of the junction for the extension to Blakeney, authorised in 1880 but abandoned in 1888. The area was opened up for ballast extraction in 1901 and remained in use until 1939, access being controlled from a ground frame. Local instructions warned guards of steep gradients within the sidings.

13.　Goods traffic on the branch ceased at the end of 1964, and the track from Melton Constable to Weybourne was lifted. By 1988 the North Norfolk Railway had been able to rebuild the line southwest from Weybourne, but the construction of the Holt bypass forced the company to build a new terminus on the outskirts of Holt. Class B12 4-6-0 no. 8572 stands at the single platform on the bitterly cold afternoon of 3rd March 1995, at the end of its first day in traffic since the early 1960s. (R.J.Adderson)

lling Heath
Siding

Gravel Pits

14.   Shortly after leaving Holt, the line turns to run parallel to the coast, and passengers in this train starting the tortuous descent of 1 in 80 to Weybourne station will have fine views of the sea for the next three miles or so to Sheringham. Photographed in June 1957, the engine is no 43150, one of the Ivatt class 4 2-6-0s which handled much of the traffic on the M&GN during its last decade. (Ted Tuddenham/Peter J Bower and M&GN Circle).

15.   The North Norfolk Railway's Andrew Barclay 0-6-0T no. 13 *Harlaxton* was repainted in the M&GN's "golden gorse" colour scheme and given the number 100 to mark the Centenary of the Joint Committee in 1993. It is seen here tackling the climb out of Weybourne with a demonstration freight train on 11th September that year. The engine was not entirely suited to the increasingly heavy passenger trains on the railway, and moved to pastures new after the 1996 season. (R.J.Adderson)

KELLING HEATH PARK

16.   After operating between Sheringham and Weybourne for several years, the North Norfolk Railway extended their diesel railbus service to Kelling Camp Halt in August 1983. The original rudimentary boarding place was improved and renamed Kelling Heath Park by the time services to Holt were restored. Preserved class 37 no. D6732 coasts towards the platform and its impressive nameboard on 8th November 1997.(R.J.Adderson)

4241

2nd-SINGLE   SINGLE-2nd

Holt to

Holt   Holt
Melton Constable   Melton Constable

MELTON CONSTABLE

(E)   1/6   Fare   1/6   (E)

For conditions see over   For conditions see over

4241

226

Mid. & Gt. Northern Jt. Committee
CHILD
EXCHANGE TICKET.
FOR CONDITIONS SEE BACK.

H O L T to
SHERINGHAM
Available only on date shewn hereon.
Not available intermediately or for break of
Journey. Issued in exchange for return half of
Eastern Counties Omnibus Co.'s ticket.

THIRD

226

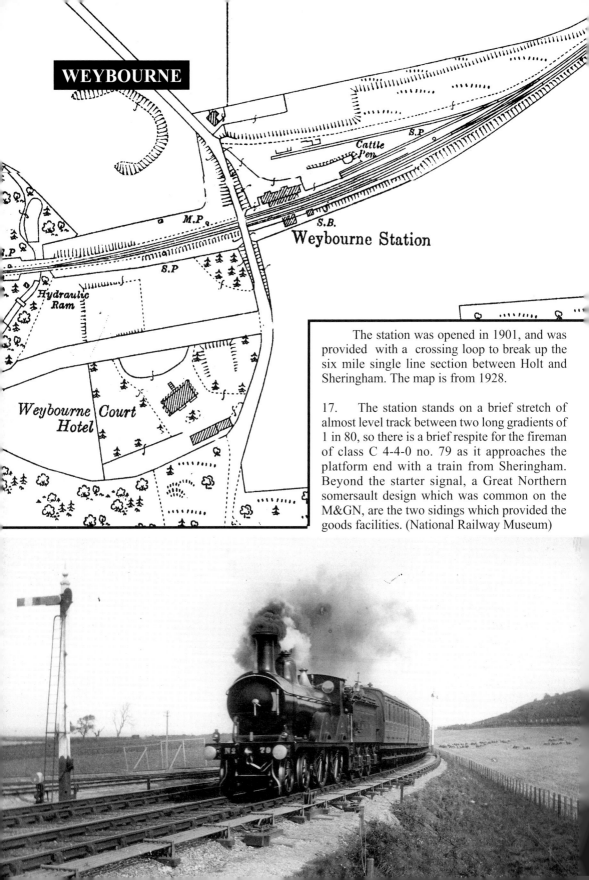

WEYBOURNE

Weybourne Station

Hydraulic Ram

Weybourne Court Hotel

The station was opened in 1901, and was provided with a crossing loop to break up the six mile single line section between Holt and Sheringham. The map is from 1928.

17. The station stands on a brief stretch of almost level track between two long gradients of 1 in 80, so there is a brief respite for the fireman of class C 4-4-0 no. 79 as it approaches the platform end with a train from Sheringham. Beyond the starter signal, a Great Northern somersault design which was common on the M&GN, are the two sidings which provided the goods facilities. (National Railway Museum)

18. Looking west, the view of the station has changed little since this picture was taken in 1924. Although British Railways demolished both the signal box and the waiting shelter on the up platform, replacement structures have been built which preserve the atmosphere. (Stations UK)

19. Seen from the road bridge, the hilly and wooded surroundings are apparent as class C 4-4-0 no. 012 runs into the station with a stopping train from Melton Constable in 1938. The train is formed of two LNWR bogie coaches, followed by GNR and M&GN six-wheelers, with a fitted van at the rear. Such a cosmopolitan collection was typical at the time. (The late P.A.Vicary)

20. After working a troop train to Weybourne, class B17 4-6-0 no. 1601 *Holkham* came to grief at the end of the headshunt (the upper track on the right of the map) on 1st October 1948. Nobody was hurt and as the main line was not blocked the loco was left where it was until the following Sunday, when the Norwich breakdown gang was sent to the scene. It took a full day's work to get the engine back on the rails. (D.Daniels)

21.   The driver of an Ivatt class 4 2-6-0 leans from his cab one day in the 1950s as another engine of the same class rolls down the hill into the station. He will be on his way again as soon as the single track to Holt is clear. (J.E.Levick)

22.   The up loop was removed following closure of the signalbox on 6th June 1961 and by mid - 1965 the remaining track had been lifted through the platforms. At this time, the fortunes of the station were at their lowest point. (K.M.Mills)

23.   The driver of NNR's Waggon und Maschinenbau diesel railbus no. E79963 collects the token for the section to Holt as the crew of the replica *Rocket* looks on. The steam locomotive was making a brief visit to the railway when this picture was taken on 31st July 1993, whilst the railbus was amongst the first arrivals on the preserved line in 1967. (R.J.Adderson)

24.   The facilities, and indeed the train services, have increased out of all recognition in the preservation era. This busy scene on 5th September 1997 shows the station on the left, where class 37 no. D6732 is waiting for Hunslet 0-6-0T no. 3809 to clear the single line from Sheringham. The loco shed, works and yard are in the centre, whilst a trail of smoke on the hillside indicates another train clambering up the bank towards Holt. (R.J.Adderson)

15

EAST OF WEYBOURNE - BRIDGE 303

25.   The bridge carrying the line over the A149 coast road is a popular place for enthusiasts to watch activity on the preserved line. On the final afternoon of BR passenger services though, the photographer was entirely alone to record the passing of the 2.12 pm train from Norwich. The marker posts to the right of the picture indicate the 5 mph. speed restriction resulting from the poor condition of the bridge. (R.J.Adderson)

26.   Just over thirteen years later, enthusiasts have arrived by car and coach to see the newly restored class J15 0-6-0 no. 564 cautiously crossing the bridge on its way to Sheringham. (D.C.Pearce)

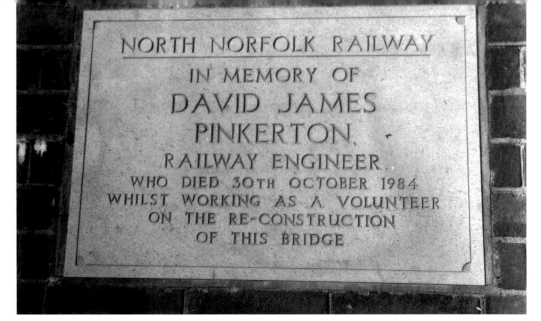

NORTH NORFOLK RAILWAY
IN MEMORY OF
DAVID JAMES
PINKERTON,
RAILWAY ENGINEER.
WHO DIED 30TH OCTOBER 1984
WHILST WORKING AS A VOLUNTEER
ON THE RE-CONSTRUCTION
OF THIS BRIDGE

27.   It was necessary to strengthen bridge 303 before the speed restriction could be removed. Sadly, David Pinkerton, a professional railwayman working as a volunteer, died in an accident while work was in progress. This plaque on the bridge abutment is a lasting monument. (G.L.Kenworthy)

28.   The extent of the rebuilding work is evident as the J15 crosses the bridge with a train for Weybourne on August Bank Holiday Monday, 1985. By this time the locomotive had been repainted in its LNER guise as no. 7564. (D.C.Pearce)

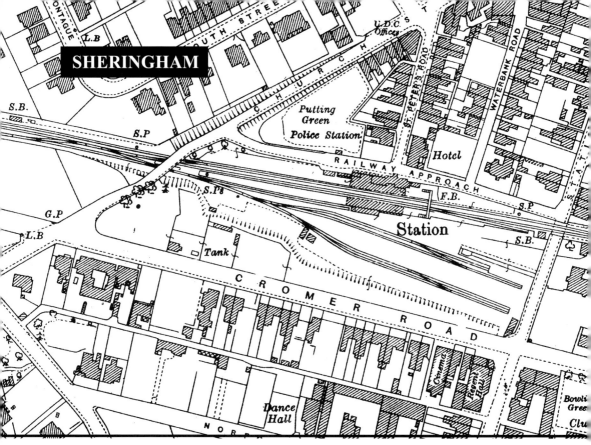

The original signal box at the centre of the station was replaced in 1906 by two new boxes, "East" and "West", to cope with additional traffic. The map date is 1928.

29.   Whilst the menfolk play golf on the links beyond the line, the two children are far more interested in the photographer than the everyday sight of class A 4-4-0 no. 29 steaming past at the head of a string of six-wheel coaches. The five lamp irons on the smokebox date the picture between 1894 and 1903. (National Railway Museum)

30.   The original signal box, a lofty structure providing an unobstructed view over the station buildings, is a feature of this early view looking eastwards. The buildings on the right hand platform were demolished during the 1960s; those on the left were little changed externally in 1998. (R.H.Clark)

31.   This old carriage was the summer house of William Marriott and stood in the garden of his residence overlooking Sheringham station. Marriott worked for the M&GN and its predecessors from 1880 until his retirement at the end of 1924, holding the posts of engineer from 1883, and loco supcrintcndcnt from 1884. In addition to these responsibilities, he was appointed traffic manager in January 1919. (Courtesy Anglia TV, NNR and M&GN Circle)

32.   On a hot August day in 1955, class D16/3 4-4-0 no. 62578, immaculately turned out by Melton Constable shed, stands in Sheringham station with inspection saloon No. E942090. The coach survived in BR service until 1968, and was preserved on the Bluebell Railway in Sussex. (W.J.Naunton)

←⎯⎯⎯⎯⎯⎯

33.   The diesel train from Norwich appears to have done a good trade as a number of alighting passengers make their way to the footbridge on 28th February 1959. The destination blind is correct, as the train is on a through working from Norwich (Thorpe) to Norwich (City). On the far platform, the bookstall and mobile magazine trolley are worthy of note. (A.E.Bennett)

34.   A train of empty wagons passes between the West box and the carriage siding behind Brush Type 2 no. D5566 on 6th September 1960. This train too is making the long haul between the two Norwich stations, but from the following Monday such workings would avoid the Sheringham area following the opening of a new connecting line at Themelthorpe. (B.Harrison)

35.   By the mid 1960s the station was far too large for BR's needs, and a new halt was opened on the east side of the level crossing on 2nd January 1967. The track over the crossing remained in place, enabling a train of stock to be delivered directly to the infant preservation society on 4th June 1967. Type 2 no. D5533 was photographed returning to Norwich after this working. The halt is in the foreground, whilst the buffer stops have been removed temporarily to allow the train to pass. (R.J.Adderson)

36.   The East signalbox seen in the previous picture was subsequently moved to the station platform where it can be seen on 23rd October 1977. The crowds are out in force to see class J15 0-6-0 no. 564, formerly BR no. 65462, on its first weekend in traffic following a long overhaul. (B.Harrison)

37.   A through train from London to Sheringham continued to run on summer Saturdays until 1975. This final descendant of the "Norfolk Coast Express", a six-car rake of Cravens DMUs normally employed on Kings Cross suburban services, stands at the buffer stops on 22nd August 1970, having arrived as the 10.04 a.m. from Liverpool Street. By this time the line to the original station had been removed. (Geoff Pember Bequest/GERS coll.)

38.   Since 1993, the Sprinter units have virtually monopolised the train service to Sheringham from Norwich. Single car no. 153311 stands at the basic platform in the autumn of 1997. (G.L.Kenworthy)

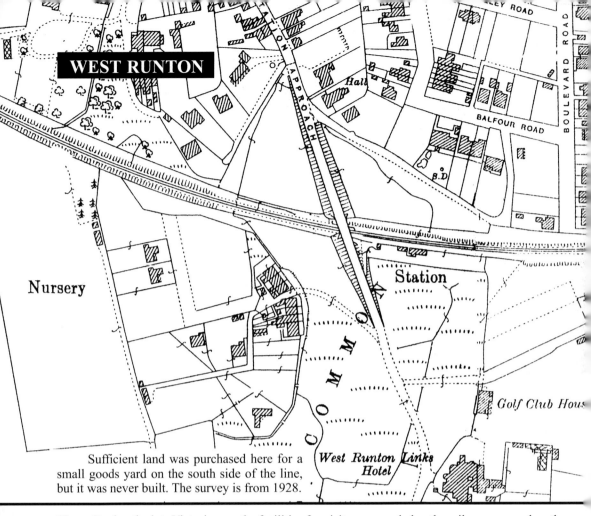

WEST RUNTON

Hall

BALFOUR ROAD

Nursery

Station

COMMON

Golf Club House

Sufficient land was purchased here for a small goods yard on the south side of the line, but it was never built. The survey is from 1928.

West Runton Links Hotel

39.   During the late Victorian era the facilities for visitors expanded as the railways opened up the North Norfolk coast. The large hotel in the background of this view was typical of many that sprang up in the coastal towns and villages between Mundesley and Weybourne during this period. The station facilities though, are considerably less prestigious! (G.L.Kenworthy coll.)

WEST RUNTON

40.   Before the World War I, the West Runton stop was used to collect tickets from passengers bound for Cromer on certain trains. This procedure seems to be taking place here – one can imagine the railway employee calling "Cromer tickets please" as he strides along the platform, and the passengers peering from the carriage windows in response. The driver of class C 4-4-0 no. 79 seems quite philosophical about the protracted stop. (National Railway Museum)

41.   With the North Sea in the background, a class 153 skirts the golf course between West Runton station and the site of Runton West Junction on 22nd October 1997. (G.L.Kenworthy)

Way out →

42.   In the 1990s the concrete nameboard and wooden fencing still provided a tangible link with M&GN days. Sprinter no. 156401 makes a brief stop with a train for Sheringham on 2nd July 1993. (R.J.Adderson)

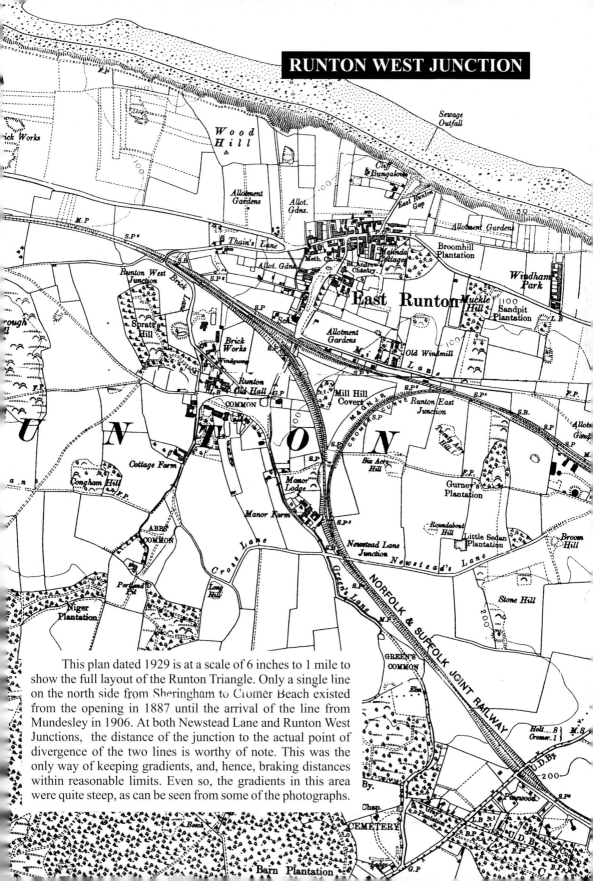

This plan dated 1929 is at a scale of 6 inches to 1 mile to show the full layout of the Runton Triangle. Only a single line on the north side from Sheringham to Cromer Beach existed from the opening in 1887 until the arrival of the line from Mundesley in 1906. At both Newstead Lane and Runton West Junctions, the distance of the junction to the actual point of divergence of the two lines is worthy of note. This was the only way of keeping gradients, and, hence, braking distances within reasonable limits. Even so, the gradients in this area were quite steep, as can be seen from some of the photographs.

43. In September 1960 the track layout at Runton West Junction was intact, even though the line to Newstead Lane carried freight traffic only. The original M&GN route to Cromer is on the right, and beyond the bridge the four tracks converge into one as far as Sheringham. (B.Harrison)

44. We now take the line into Cromer Beach station as a Derby lightweight DMU heads towards Runton East Junction in the late 1950s. The bridge and signal box at Runton West provide a link with the previous picture, but already the difference in levels between the two lines is noticeable. (Norfolk Railway Society Archive)

45.   Two viaducts dominate the otherwise rural village of East Runton. In October 1997 a
Sheringham to Cromer train crosses the more northerly viaduct, whilst the nearer one had not seen
any trains for well over thirty years. (G.L.Kenworthy)

RUNTON EAST JUNCTION

The Gas Works siding was completed in 1899, but the layout shown in this 1928 survey dates from 1905 when the line from Runton East Junction to Cromer Beach was doubled in connection with the openings of 1906.

46.　　Shortly after the LNER take-over, a stopping train from Cromer Beach is signalled on to the Sheringham line at Runton East Junction. Renumbered 041 by its new owners, the 4-4-2T would survive only another seven or eight years, being withdrawn in 1944, but the distinctive double-posted signal gantry was to control the junction for another quarter of a century. (E.G.P. Masterman / Coll. R.Monk)

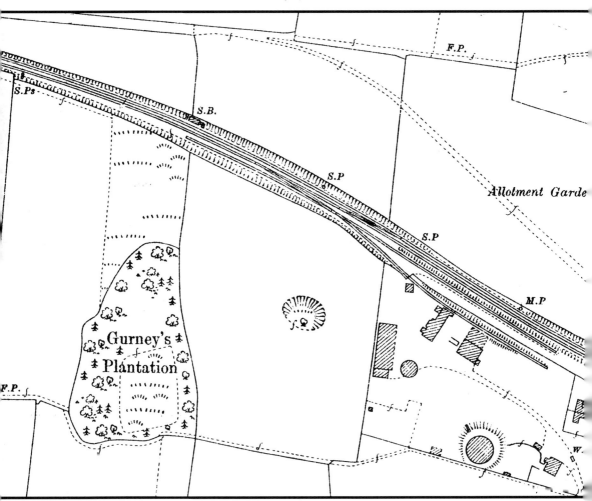

1937 Appendix

GAS WORKS SIDING BETWEEN RUNTON EAST JUNCTION AND CROMER.

Owing to the falling gradient, Goods trains from Cromer must, on arrival at the Gas Works Siding, be placed therein clear of the line leading to and from the Siding and the Main line. Traffic from the Gas Works must be marshalled on the brake in the Siding.

47.   After rationalisation, Cromer was approached from Runton East on two parallel single tracks. Running on the line from Sheringham, a Class 150 passes the site of the former gasworks siding on this stretch in the autumn of 1997. (G.L.Kenworthy)

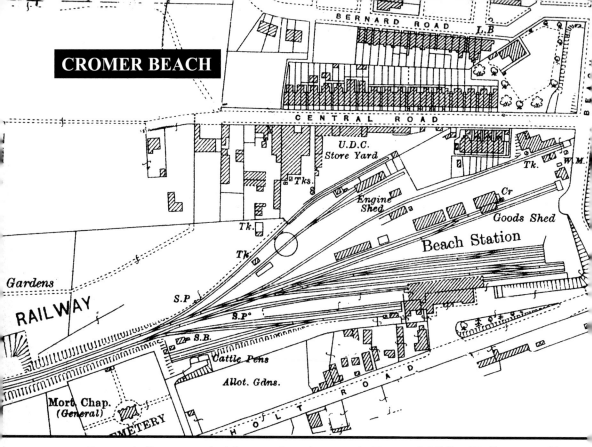

CROMER BEACH

Because its line approached the town from the west, the Eastern & Midland Railway was able to select a site for its station closer to the town and the beach than that of the GER. This is the layout in 1928.

48.   Passengers gather on the platform on a hot summer morning in the early years of the twentieth century. Whilst the railway enthusiast will note the initials EMR entwined in the end of the seat and the original tall signal box beyond the platform end, the ladies' fashions, their parasols and the picnic hamper being loaded into the train are no less worthy of note. (R.J.Adderson coll.)

MIDLAND & Gᵗ NORTHERN JOINT RAILWAY		
CHEAP DAY TRIPS.		
EACH WEEK DAY.	*Mons Weds & Saturday* NORFOLK BROADS	*TUES & THURS.*
SHERINGHAM 6	STALHAM 1/11 POTTER HEIGHAM 2 5 YARMOUTH 3 11	NORWICH 3/-
OVERSTRAND 5	LOWESTOFT 5 3	Wednesdays for SANDRINGHAM.
TRIMINGHAM 9	*Mons Weds & Fridays* HOLT 1 3	HILLINGTON 4/9
MUNDESLEY 1 0	WEYBOURNE 10	KINGS LYNN 5 8

49.   The M&GN did its best to attract custom from the holidaymakers in the area, as this poster board outside Cromer station around 1930 testifies. (William C.Fulcher coll./M&GN Circle)

50.   One of the handsome M&GN 4-4-2 tank locomotives, no. 20, waits in the bay platform with a local train in 1929. (H.C.Casserley)

51.   Class F6 2-4-2T no. 67228 stands at the buffer stops on 6th April 1953, having worked the 10.05 a.m. train from North Walsham via Overstrand, on the last day of services over the N&S route. A comparison with picture 48 will reveal that the lighting has not changed during the previous half century. (B.Harrison)

52.   The M&GN station at Cromer was a dignified building, and when this picture was taken on 2nd September 1959, it still boasted a refreshment room as well as full station facilities. Redundant after the introduction of conductor-guard working, the building was under threat of demolition for some time, but following extensive restoration, opened its doors again as a public house in June 1998. (Geoff Pember Bequest/ GERS coll.)

53.   This general view from the platform end on 28th February 1959 shows the carriage sidings, loco shed and goods yard, as well as the passenger station. The platform had been lengthened as part of the improvements made to handle the extra traffic resulting from the closure of High station in 1954. (Laurie Ward/M&GN Circle)

54.   Inevitably the overall roof tended to make the far end of the platform a dark and gloomy place. Just occasionally though, as on the evening of 20th July 1963, the sun would shine directly along the platform and pick out the details under the canopy. The train departure board tells us that the Derby lightweight unit is about to work an all stations train to Norwich Thorpe.
(Richard T Ninnis/M&GN Circle)

55.   Again the afternoon sun makes for dramatic lighting as a four-car DMU rake passes the squat replacement signal box (see original in picture 48) in the early 1960s, whilst a Brush Type 2 waits to leave on a goods train.
(The late P.A.Vicary)

56.   This is the road entrance to the goods yard, looking west in 1964. Several wagons stand in the sidings, whilst the goods shed and crane are prominent. Cromer ceased to handle general freight traffic in April 1966, but a regular coal train continued to use the yard until 31st January 1969. (Geoff Pember Bequest/GERS coll.)

57.   Here we have another picture from the early diesel era. The gentlemen's fashions are in their way just as distinctive as those in picture 48, whilst a comparison with picture 54 makes us wonder just what logic led to the renumbering of the platforms! (R.F.Bonny)

Mid. & G.N.J'nt Committee
Issued subject to the conditions & regulations in
the Cos Time Tables Books Bills & Notices &in the
Railway Cos Book of regulations relating to traffic
by Passenger train or other similar service
------ C H I L D ------
CROMER (BEACH) TO
SHERINGHAM
3999
THIRD
CLASS

58.   During 1991 a supermarket was built on the land previously occupied by the railway yards. Somewhat hemmed in by the new development, class 20 no. 20901 *Nancy* stands at the platform with the weedkiller train, making its annual visit on 17th September 1994. (D.C.Pearce)

2. Runton West Junction to North Walsham Town

RUNTON WEST JUNCTION
TO NEWSTEAD LANE JUNCTION

59.   Having reached Cromer Beach by the M&GN route, we now retrace our steps to Runton West Junction, the western extremity of the N&S route, which we shall follow to North Walsham. Seen from the brake van of a Norwich (City) to Trowse goods train on 10th September 1960, class WD 2-8-0 no. 90709 is just crossing the viaduct seen in picture 45. (B.Harrison)

60.   Thirty-seven years on, and weeds and undergrowth have replaced the well-tended track over Runton viaduct. A class 153 crosses the M&GN viaduct on its way to Sheringham. (R.J.Adderson)

61.   Half a mile or so beyond the viaduct, no. 90709 is seen again as it passes Newstead Lane Junction signal box. The lines on the left form the third side of the Cromer triangle to Runton East Junction. (B.Harrison)

62.   We break our journey to Mundesley to look at the third side of the triangle. As this is part of the surviving route to Cromer, it is entirely appropriate to show class B12 4-6-0 no. 61514 curving round to Newstead Lane with a train from Cromer to London on 25th April 1956. The line from Runton West is on the left of the picture. (The late P.A.Vicary)

63.   Another through London train, this time the 12.30 p.m. from Liverpool Street, approaches Runton East on 14th September 1957 behind class B12 4-6-0 no. 61519. This picture is notable in featuring all three lines of the triangle, with the Runton East to Runton West lines in the foreground and a signal on the avoiding line to the right of the train. (B.Harrison)

64.   On a September afternoon in 1960 the signalman at Newstead Lane returns to his box having handed over the token for the single-track section to Roughton Road. As at Runton West, four running lines converged into one at this spot. (B.Harrison)

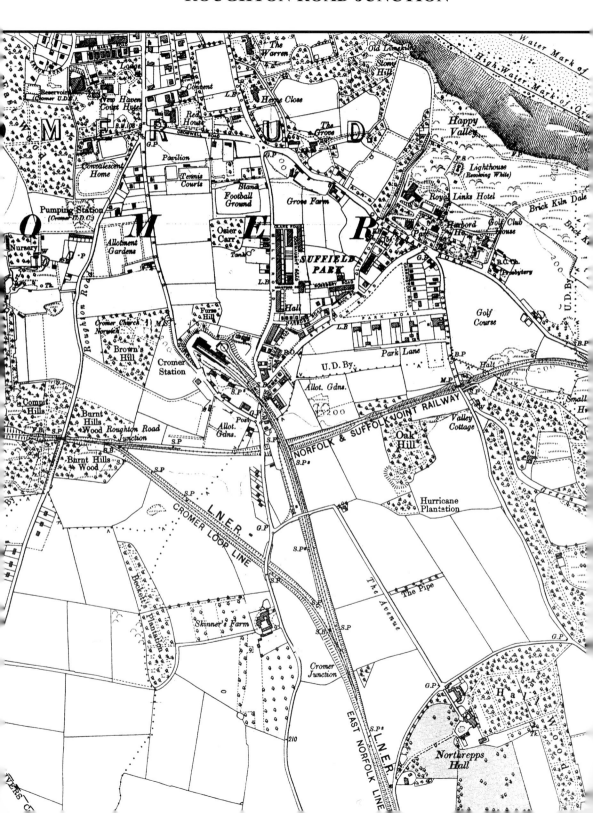

65.   The signal box at Roughton Road Junction was a most distinctive building with its hipped roof. The GE line to Cromer Junction, just beyond the distant road bridge, curves sharply to the right at this point, while the trackbed of the N&S route to Mundesley continues straight on. (R.F.Bonny)

66.   A lightweight goods train takes the curve past the signal box on 9th May 1959 behind class J39 0-6-0 no. 64761. (R.Harrison)

        This is a 6 inches to 1 mile plan, dated 1928, illustrating the whole layout in this area. It includes Roughton Road Junction, the point at which the GE line to Cromer Junction left the N&S loop line towards Mundesley, and also the site of the halt opened in 1985 on the south side of the line. To the east of the junction the modest length, 62 yards, of Norfolk's only tunnel is evident, as is the convenience of the halt for the golf course; how much use was made of it by the golfing fraternity is another matter. From 1906 until 1954 Cromer Junction was the point where through coaches for Sheringham were detached from GE section trains for the final part of their journey. More significantly, it was the point from which trains from the Sheringham direction were propelled into Cromer High station before resuming their journey towards Norwich. This manoeuvre, over a distance of more than ½ mile, had few parallels anywhere in the country. Cromer High station is also shown; this will be visited in more detail later.

67. A new station was opened at Roughton Road on 20th May 1985 to serve housing developments in the area. The site of the junction has vanished beneath the trees, but the curvature of the track provides a link with the previous picture, as a class 153 passes on its way to the coast in April 1998. (R.J.Adderson)

68. The Cromer area was notable for some distinctive bridges, of which this one spanning Roughton Road was a good example. The new station had not been considered when this picture was taken in the 1950s. (R.F.Bonny)

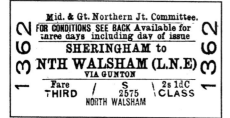

69. Bridges 326 under the Norwich Road, and 327, the tunnel under Cromer High station approaches, followed in quick succession. This picture probably dates from the mid 1950s, as the N&S trackbed is not yet overgrown. (R.F.Bonny)

CROMER LINKS HALT

70.   The halt was approached from the road by a path up the side of the embankment, seen here around the time of opening in 1923. The authors were surprised and delighted to find the rotting remains of the gate entangled in the undergrowth at the site over seventy years later!
(Ted Tuddenham /Peter J Bower and M&GN Circle)

71.   Facilities here were basic, but probably quite adequate for the traffic generated. The wooden platform, which cost £170 to build, is seen looking westwards around 1950, with the Roughton Road Junction distant signal on the left. (Stations UK)

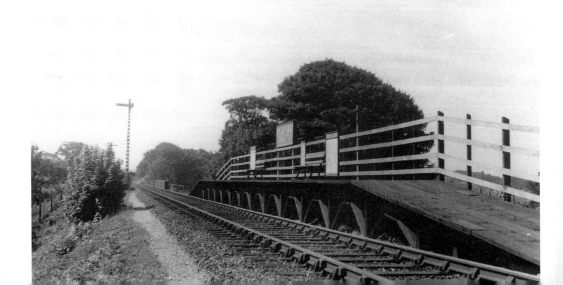

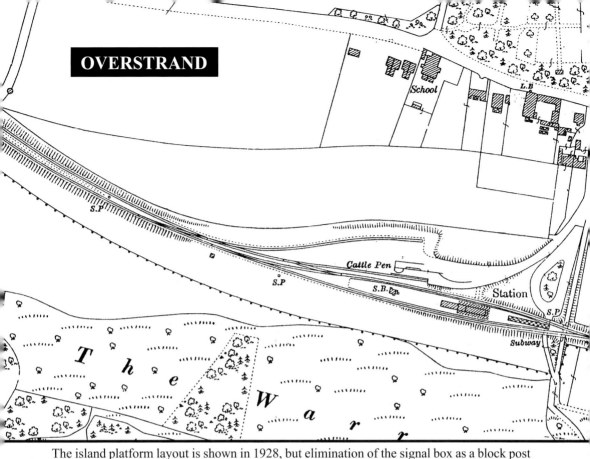

OVERSTRAND

The island platform layout is shown in 1928, but elimination of the signal box as a block post in 1922 meant that the south side platform was not used after that date, although the track was retained for some years as a siding. The scale is 20 ins to 1 mile.

72.   In contrast, the original stations on the N&S route were spacious and substantial affairs, built to cater for a holiday trade which never materialised. Seen from the south, an 0-4-4T on loan from the Midland Railway runs round its train, passing the roof of the long subway leading to the island platform. The presence of this locomotive dates the picture between 1906 and 1912. (Lens of Sutton)

73.   There is a somewhat neglected air around the place as a "last day" train pulls out past the entrance to the goods yard. Beyond the platform the distant rails can be seen climbing sharply over the undulating countryside. Later in the day, the conductor–guard sold the last ticket for a journey from Overstrand to Mr Edward Brown, who had issued the very first ticket at the station 47 years earlier. (B.Harrison)

74.   Having gone through the "Entrance for passengers", the intending traveller would turn right up the long slope to platform level. After 1922 he would have to buy his ticket on the train, although there would still be a porter on the premises, under the control of the Mundesley station master. Similar staffing arrangements applied at Trimingham and at Paston. The general untidiness confirms that this view looking west was taken after closure, but the station was little changed. (E.G.P.Masterman /R. Monk coll.)

SIDESTRAND HALT

75.   Tucked away at the end of a footpath Sidestrand Halt had a life of only some seventeen years. Although it consisted of no more than a platform edge of sleepers backed up by a surface of cinder ash everything looks very neat and tidy in this photograph taken soon after the opening of the Halt in 1936. (Norwich City Library coll./M&GN Circle).

76.   Two lady passengers watch the departing train on Easter Monday 1953, the last day of services. They would have to rely on the bus service to get them to North Walsham or Mundesley for their shopping in the months to come. (B.Harrison)

TRIMINGHAM

An O.S. plan showing the station layout has proved elusive. Although the station was opened in 1906, the same year as the survey, the tracks had not been laid when the surveyor visited the site.

77.   In 1950, this ancient tender was in use as a water tank, tucked away at the end of a siding. It had outlived the former Cornwall Minerals Railway locomotive, to which it had been attached, by more than half a century. For many years a six wheeled tender performed a similar function at Overstrand. (J.E.Levick)

78.   It is easy to forget the impact that the closure of the railway had on the rural communities of the 1950s. After their "last day" ride, a group of local people say their farewells to the guard, whilst other passengers board the ex-GER coach for their final trip on the line. (Brian L Ridgway/M&GN Circle)

79.   The economies of the 1920s are reflected in this view from the train in 1953. The signal box has been replaced with a ground frame, whilst there is no track to serve the south side of the island platform. It is remarkable how the abandoned trackbed has been kept neat and tidy. (B.Harrison)

80.   Although derelict, the station was substantially intact as the 1960s dawned – even one of the nameboards survived. Within a few years though, the site was to disappear under a housing development. The corrugated iron roof was very much "state of the art" when the station was built. (P.G.Rayner)

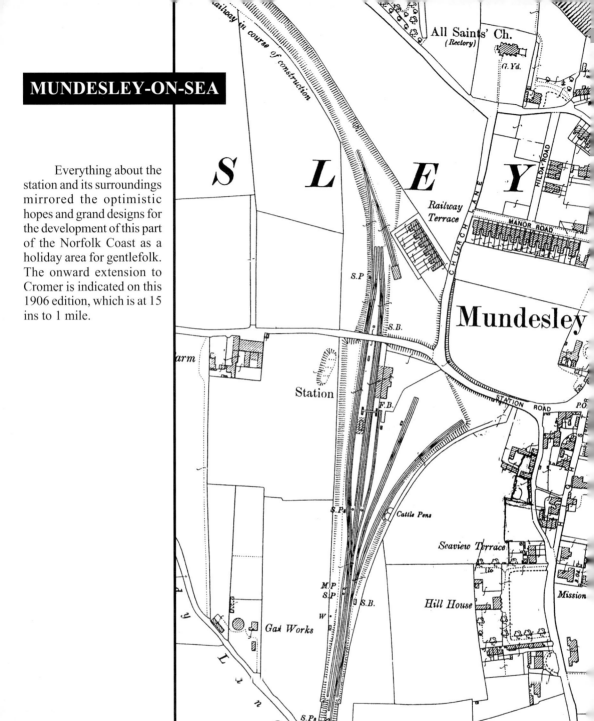

MUNDESLEY-ON-SEA

Everything about the station and its surroundings mirrored the optimistic hopes and grand designs for the development of this part of the Norfolk Coast as a holiday area for gentlefolk. The onward extension to Cromer is indicated on this 1906 edition, which is at 15 ins to 1 mile.

S   L   E   Y

All Saints' Ch.
(Rectory)
G. Yd.

Railway
Terrace

Mundesley

arm

Station

Seaview Terrace

Hill House

Mission

Gas Works

Cattle Pens

1937 Appendix

MUNDESLEY.

An auxiliary tablet instrument is fixed in a cabin at the north end of the Down platform for the withdrawal or cancellation of tablets for the Mundesley–Roughton Road Junction section when necessary for the expeditious working of trains, and Drivers may hand to or receive a tablet from the member of the station staff deputed for the duty.

81.   All the hopes and aspirations of the builders are evident in this early view looking south towards North Walsham. As well as the three through platforms, a bay was provided beyond the footbridge. (National Railway Museum)

82.   With its clock tower, half-timbered gables, balustrades and spacious forecourt, the exterior of the station was equally impressive. (Mrs J.Moore)

83.   Even if the anticipated prosperity never occurred, the railway certainly played its part in the life of the town, as this busy 1958 scene testifies. (Stations UK)

84.   A locomotive shed had been provided when the line was constructed, but was a very short-lived facility. The large water tank however, supported on massive timbers, survived until the station closed, and adds interest to this picture of class J15 0-6-0 no. 65469 on a special working for the Norfolk Railway Society on 15th May 1960. (B.Harrison)

85.   As at West Runton, a large hotel dominates the skyline as we look north along the somewhat neglected looking platforms on 29th August 1964. A Derby lightweight DMU waits to leave for North Walsham, whilst a connecting bus waits in the station forecourt. No fewer than six camping coaches are parked in the platforms. (Geoff Pember Bequest/GERS coll.)

86.   The track on the west side of the island platform had been lifted between the wars, but an isolated length was later relaid to accommodate the camping coaches. It is said that this was one of the greatest concentrations of camping coaches in the country. (Mrs J.Moore)

PASTON & KNAPTON

The rudimentary nature of the track and signalling facilities contrasted with the somewhat generous, not to say grandiose, appearance of the station buildings. This is the 1906 survey.

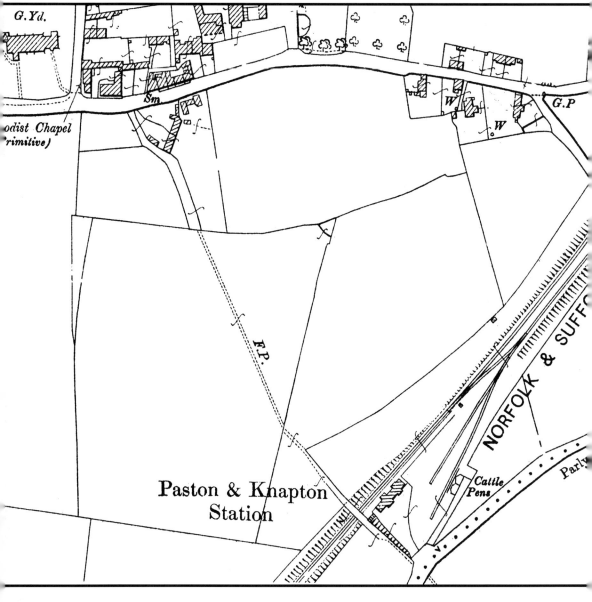

G.Yd.

odist Chapel
rimitive)

Sm.

W

W

G.P

FP.

Paston & Knapton
Station

NORFOLK & SUFFO

Cattle
Pens

Parly

87.   The pristine brickwork of the station building and the fresh white paint on the gates show
that the station has only just been built, whilst the horse and trap in the yard are a further sign of
more leisurely times. (National Railway Museum)

88.   By 29th August 1964 the station was unstaffed, under threat of closure and its rather run
down appearance from the platform reflected this sad situation. The concrete nameboard survived
to the end. (Geoff Pember Bequest/GERS coll.)

89.   The reason why goods trains continued to run for some three months after the passenger closure is clearly shown in this October 1964 picture. At least eight trucks of sugar beet occupy the yard, probably destined for one of the large factories in the area such as Wissington, Cantley, or Kings Lynn. (Ted Tuddenham/Peter J Bower and M&GN Circle).

90.   Proudly bearing an "express passenger" headcode, class J15 0-6-0 no. 65469 pauses with a special train organised by the Norfolk Railway Society on 15th May 1960 to provide its members with driving and firing experience. The small ground frame cabin controlling the entrance to the goods yard can be seen at the far end of the platform. (J.E.Levick)

ANTINGHAM ROAD JUNCTION

This was the point at which the GE line from North Walsham Main joined the M&GN line from North Walsham Town to form the N&S line onwards towards Mundesley. It was another location, along with Runton West Junction and Newstead Lane Junction, where four tracks ran into one. The map date is 1928.

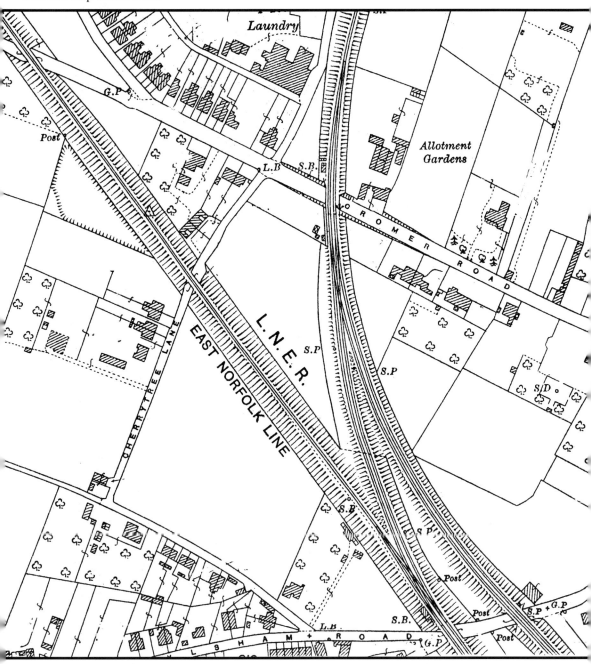

91.   This view of the junction at Antingham Road was taken from the rear of a North Walsham Main to Mundesley and Cromer train on 6th April 1953. The line to the M&GN station runs off to the left, whilst the direct GE line to Cromer can be seen on the embankment beyond the coach. By this time services to the Mundesley line were concentrated on the GE station. (B.Harrison)

PASSENGER WORKING ARRANGEMENTS

10.50 a.m. SO Liverpool Street to Caister-on-Sea.

After the M.G.N. Section engine has been attached and the incoming engine has been uncoupled the Driver of the latter must after Rule 133 Clause (c) has been carried out, assist the train to the Antingham Road Jc. Advance Starting Signal to M.G.N. Section.

10.40 a.m. SO Caister-on-Sea to Liverpool Street.

After the oncoming engine has been attached and the M.G.N. Section engine has been detached, the Driver of the latter must after Rule 133, Clause (c) has been carried out, assist the train to North Walsham Main Outer Home Signal.

92.   Latterly the only regular passenger train to use the connection to the M&GN station was the "Holiday Camps Express" which ran on Summer Saturdays from Liverpool Street to Caister on Sea. The main line locomotive has drawn the coaches forward from the GE line on to the single-track section, and a J17 0-6-0 has backed on to what was the rear of the train for the last part of the journey, over the M&GN route to Caister. The replacement engine is struggling to get its heavy train on the move, but hopefully the main line engine will be providing assistance as laid down in the Working Timetable. (J.E.Levick)

93.   The little-used connection to the M&GN was abandoned from 8th April 1958 owing to the condition of an underbridge, and no time was wasted in lifting the tracks. By August of that year only the trackbed remained, running to the site of the former junction by the signal box. The GE connection had also been reduced to single track as part of the remodelling of the layout here. (A.E.Bennett)

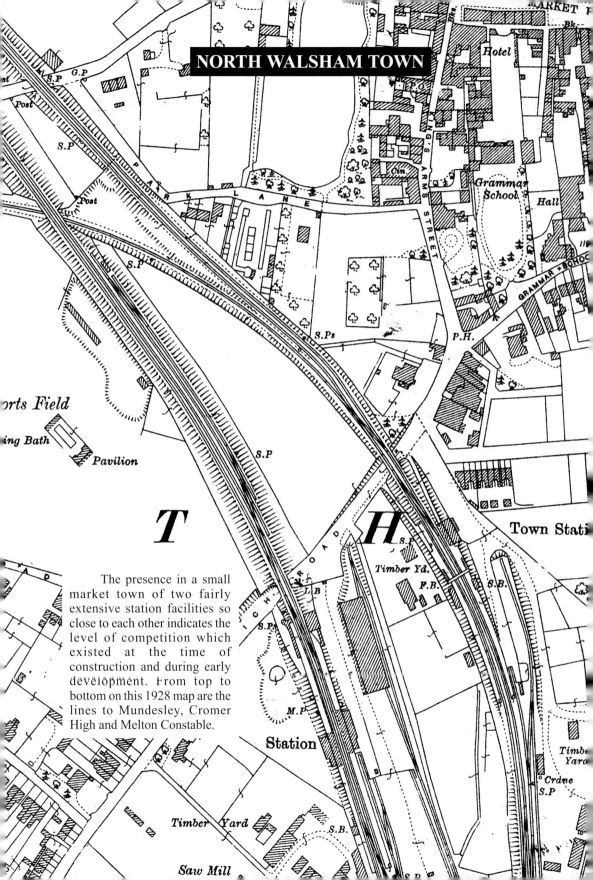

NORTH WALSHAM TOWN

Hotel

King's Arms Street

Grammar School

Hall

Grammar School

P.H.

Sports Field

ing Bath

Pavilion

S.P

T

H

S.Ps

Timber Yd.

F.B.

S.B.

Town Stati

The presence in a small market town of two fairly extensive station facilities so close to each other indicates the level of competition which existed at the time of construction and during early development. From top to bottom on this 1928 map are the lines to Mundesley, Cromer High and Melton Constable.

M.P.

Station

Timb Yard

Crane S.P

Timber Yard

Saw Mill

S.B.

94.　　Looking east, the buildings, signalling and lighting appear to be complete in this picture dating from early 1883, shortly before the line to Melton was opened. A Class B 4-4-0T is partially obscured by the fencing. (Marriott coll./M&GN Circle)

95.　　North of the station, milepost 0 indicates the starting point of the mileage on the Mundesley line. Together with the adjacent gradient post, it was a typical concrete product of Melton Constable works. (R.F.Bonny)

96. The down "Holiday Camps Express" from Liverpool Street approaches North Walsham station from Antingham Road Junction behind class 4 2-6-0 no. 43160 on 7th September 1957. (B.Harrison)

97. Looking west from the footbridge, the M&GN line to Melton Constable is seen curving to the left down the gradient, with the double track to Antingham Road Junction diverging beyond the bridge over the road. Class 4 2-6-0 no. 43160 is arriving with a local train from Melton Constable. (D.Lawrence)

98.   Rearrangement of the track layout in the Spring of 1958 was a labour intensive process. A new starter signal has been erected by the road bridge and the arms and bracket of the old junction signal have been removed prior to demolition. On completion of the work, only the first hundred yards or so of the up line to Antingham Road remained as a siding.
(Deryck Featherstone/M&GN Circle)

99.   We now leave the M&GN to take the GE route back to Cromer. This last glimpse of Town station was taken from a train on the parallel GE line on 28th February 1959. (A.E.Bennett)

3. North Walsham Main to Cromer High

NORTH WALSHAM MAIN

100.   The two railways serving North Walsham are linked by these surviving items. The station seat is of a design which was provided when the M&GN station opened, and which appears in picture 97, whilst the headboards were carried by the prestige expresses which ran from Liverpool Street to Cromer and Sheringham in the 1950s. (G.L.Kenworthy)

101.   LNER Restaurant Car no. 672 was photographed on 9th May 1931 bearing the "Liverpool Street & Cromer" roofboards. This vehicle was built at Stratford in 1918 as a kitchen and sick officers' car for United States Ambulance Train no. 75. After the war it was repurchased by the GER from the War Department and in January 1920 was converted to restaurant car no. 67, with a kitchen and a dining compartment for twenty 1st class passengers. It became LNER no. 672 and was used on East Anglian main line trains until the 1950s, before transfer to the Scottish Region and final withdrawal on 31st December 1962. (National Railway Museum)

102.   Both the station staff and the loco crew pose for the photographer by the original station buildings in the 1880s. A Sinclair Y class 2-4-0 heads the goods train. (Marriott coll./M&GN Circle)

103.   There are plenty of passengers for the Norwich train as it arrives from Cromer on a wet day in 1958. At this time the station was still lit by gas lamps. (Stations UK)

104.   As the station stood on an embankment, a subway from the ground level booking office led to the platforms. With the booking office entrance on the left, a Derby heavyweight DMU, a rare visitor to the area, arrives from Cromer in June 1969. An Eastern Counties "LC" has replaced the train as the connection for Mundesley. (G.H.Smith)

105.   Tubs of flowers brighten the platforms, but the brick built station buildings are looking decidedly scruffy as the weedkiller train arrives from the south on 11th July 1997. These buildings were demolished early in 1998 but some of the ironwork was incorporated in the replacement shelters. The tower in the background belongs to a canning factory, a once typical business of Norfolk market towns.(R.J.Adderson)

106.   GER "Claud Hamilton" 4-4-0 no. 1875 has just left North Walsham for Cromer and approaches the junction with the Mundesley line. The embankment of the line from the M&GN station to Antingham Road Junction can be seen through the arch of the bridge. (B.Adams coll.)

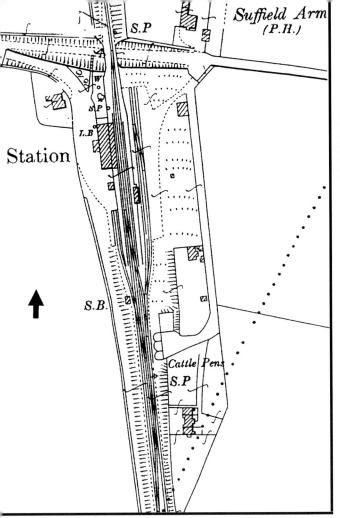

GUNTON

The station name and the generosity of platform facilities reflect the influence of Lord Suffield, a supporter of the East Norfolk Railway, whose country seat was at Gunton Park. The station is actually located in the parish of Thorpe Market and is shown on the 1906 survey.

107. This is a general view of the station looking south in 1924. The three arch bridge in the distance, no. 392, carried nothing more than a farm track and was demolished in 1945. (Stations UK)

108. Class J39 0-6-0 no. 64761 blows off steam as it stands in the small yard on the up side with a pick up goods train on 9th May 1959. Freight facilities were withdrawn from 19th April 1965. (R.Harrison)

109. By 1997 the substantial station building had been converted to a private dwelling with the nameboard reflecting the owners' efforts to recreate the railway atmosphere. On a fine October day, a class 150 leaves the short section of the former up platform still used by Anglia Railways. (G.L.Kenworthy)

110.   The weather in the first three months of 1947 provided a yardstick against which future winters would be measured, and North Norfolk suffered particularly badly. Snowdrifts halted trains on the Cromer line, and this was the scene some two miles north of Gunton before services were resumed. Tons of snow removed from the tracks create an artificial cutting, dwarfing class K1/1 2-6-0 no. 61997 *MacCailin Mor* on clearance duties. (The late P.A.Vicary)

Many day trippers arriving at Cromer High enjoyed a walk to Sherringham. If they returned by rail, they were obliged to purchase this unusual ticket to a location devoid of platforms. They were not charged for being pushed from the junction into Cromer High.

THE BROADSMAN

Restaurant Car Express

SHERINGHAM, CROMER, NORWICH, IPSWICH

AND

LONDON (Liverpool Street)

WEEKDAYS

	a.m.		p.m.
Sheringham ... ... dep	6 0	London (Liverpool St.) ... dep	3 40
West Runton ... ... ,,	6 4	Ipswich ... ... arr	5 13
Overstrand ... ... ,,	6 15	Norwich (Thorpe) ... ... ,,	6 16
Trimingham ... ... ,,	6 21	Wroxham ... ... ,,	6 46
Mundesley-on-Sea ... ,,	6 27	North Walsham (Main)... ,,	6 58
Cromer (High) ... ... ,,	6 25	Cromer (High) ... ... ,,	7 15
Gunton ... ... ,,	6 35	Mundesley-on-Sea ... arr	7 14
North Walsham (Main)... ,,	6 48	Trimingham ... ... ,,	7 22
Worstead ... ... ,,	6 54	Sidestrand Halt ... ... ,,	7A26
Wroxham ... ... ,,	7 1	Overstrand ... ... ,,	7 28
Salhouse ... ... ,,	7 8	West Runton ... ... ,,	7 40
Norwich (Thorpe) ... ... ,,	7 30	Sheringham ... ... ,,	7 43
Diss ... ... ,,	7 59		
Stowmarket ... ... ,,	8 21		
Ipswich ... ... ,,	8 41		
London (Liverpool St.) ... arr	10 16		

A Calls when required.

Passengers travelling from London (Liverpool Street) by this service can reserve seats on payment of a fee of **Is. 0d.** per seat.

June to September 1950

CROMER JUNCTION

111.   A Class S69 4-6-0 heads a Liverpool Street to Cromer express on the last leg of its journey from the capital in GER days. Cromer Junction signal box can be seen to the right of the signal post. (The late P.A.Vicary)

113.   The GER and M&GN routes into Cromer were linked in 1906, after nearly twenty years of physical isolation. A freight train behind ex-WD 2-8-0 no. 90709 curves round the connecting line from Roughton Road past the Junction signal box to join the GER route on 10th September 1960. (B.Harrison)

←――――――

112.   Following the passenger closure on 20th September 1954, the line to Cromer High continued to handle freight traffic until March 1960. Looking north from the Junction on 28th February 1959, it can be seen that the track layout and signalling had been simplified during this period. The connecting line to Cromer Beach runs to the left of the signal box. (A.E.Bennett)

CROMER HIGH

Gasometers

Gas Wor

M I L L

C.R.

Storey's Hill

Cromer
Station

Posts

P

Notice Board
(Dangerous Hill)

S.P.

Post

S.P.

The remoteness of the station from the main part of
the town and the beach is clear from this plan of 1887.
What is not so clear is the difference in elevation.

114.   High on a hill overlooking the town and the North Sea, this was an imposing building, in keeping with the traffic levels that the GER hoped to attract. This picture shows the station in the very early years, with the staff posing on the wooden framed platform. (Norfolk Museums Service)

115.   Facilities were improved as traffic developed and the station canopies were extended beyond the buffers and along a substantial length of both platforms. Their protection was not needed though, when Queen Alexandra used the station on a sunny day in 1902. The onlookers show proper respect as the royal visitor is assisted from her horse-drawn carriage. (Norfolk Museums Service)

116.   In Great Eastern days, a very clean Class S69 4-6-0 no. 1525 rests outside the single-road engine shed, which stood to the east of the platforms. (The late P.A. Vicary)

117.   For many years this magnificent signal gantry controlled traffic in and out of the station. It was replaced only a few years before the 1954 closure. (Geoff Pember Bequest/GERS coll.)

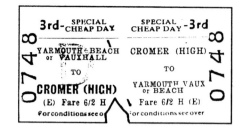

118.   The closure resulted not from lack of custom but from an entirely reasonable business decision to concentrate traffic on one conveniently sited station. When the local press photographer visited the station just before closure, therefore, he was able to record this busy scene. Class B17 4-6-0 no. 61665 *Leicester City* waits to leave with a train for Norwich, whilst a sister engine is one of the two locomotives outside the shed, partially obscured by the coaches in the bay platform.
(Eastern Counties Newspapers)

119.   During its last months, the yard at Cromer High was used for sorting material recovered from the M&GN route. This was the scene on 24th August 1959, with piles of redundant rails in the foreground and stacks of complete track panels beyond. The station water tower is prominent on the left, and behind that is the distant North Sea. (Geoff Pember Bequest/GERS coll.)

120.   On arrival at the Great Eastern station, the unsuspecting passenger might well think that his journey had finished, but there was still a long way to go! This card entitled "Cromer from the Station", bearing an August 1905 postmark, emphasises just how far he would have to travel before reaching the distant town, clustered around the church tower. Only after taking the country lane through the fields would his journey, like ours, be over. (M.J.Clark coll.)

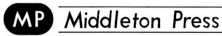

MP Middleton Press

Easebourne Lane, Midhurst
West Sussex. GU29 9AZ

A-0 906520 B-1 873793 C-1 901706 D-1 904474

OOP Out of Print at time of printing - Please check current availability **BROCHURE AVAILABLE SHOWING NEW TITLES**
Tel:01730 813169   www.middletonpress.com   email:info@middletonpress.co.uk

96